Financially Foundational Must Do's

Destiny S. Harris

. . .

. . .

Copyright

Copyright © 2024 Destiny S. Harris.

All rights reserved. No part of this publication may be reproduced without prior written permission from the author, except in the case of quotations.

Book design by Destiny S. Harris.

First printing edition 2024.

www.destinyh.com

...

. . .

A Gift For You

Thank you for taking the time to read this book. As a token of my appreciation, here is a gift to you.

I give away free books daily. Here's how to get your free books today:

Step 1: Visit

amazon.com/author/destinyharris

Step 2: Filter books by "Price: Low to High"

Step 3: Download available free eBooks

. . .

. . .

Table of Contents

. . .

. . .

Quick Bit

Thank you for taking the time to read this book.

My hope is that you leave at least 1% better than before you read this book and walk away with at least one takeaway.

I'd like to graciously ask that you help me by leaving a <u>review</u> of this book; your feedback helps me write better books and helps others get a glimpse of the book.

With Kindness,

Destiny

. . .

. . .

#1 Live Below Your Means

You can make a billion dollars per year, but you will never build wealth if you spend more than you earn.

Living below your means is the key to financial success.

Living below your means is the key to keeping money in the bank.

Living below your means is the key to building a financial purse for the future.

When you constantly spend more than you earn, you eliminate the opportunity to relieve dependence on earning income.

When you spend more than you earn, you **must** work or bring in income because you never have any, which is why most live

paycheck to paycheck.

. . .

. . .

#2 Financial Education

When you know better, you do better.

People with money lose money all the time because they don't know what to do with their money.

And you should never leave your money in someone else's hands without accountability (you).

Continuously develop an understanding of how to manage your money, even if you have a financial manager; this ensures you do not give others control of your money.

Stay in charge and stay on top of your finances through financial education.

You will inevitably create more financial

success as you acquire more financial

knowledge.

. . .

. . .

#3 Implement Boundaries

Some people don't know how to keep money because they allow everything and everyone (including themselves) to take their money as soon as they get the chance.

If you want to build wealth, you must learn how to implement boundaries and financial discipline with yourself and others.

. . .

. . .

Thank You For Reading

Thank you for reading this book.

Stay loved, blessed, lucky, favored, aware, joyous, enlightened, and committed to bettering yourself.

. . .

. . .

The End.

...

. . .

About Destiny S. Harris

Destiny S. Harris' goal is to positively inspire, cultivate, elevate, and educate the minds of individuals across the globe through her writing.

Creating (whether books, courses, articles, poetry, or music) has always been Destiny's thing, not to mention health & fitness and all things entrepreneurial.

Destiny published her first book, "Beauty Secrets for Girls," at age 11 and her second book, "Don't Wait Until It's Too Late," at age 12.

Destiny obtained three degrees in Psychology, Political Science, & Women's Studies. She also started her own music teaching business at the age of 14, which she led for over ten years. In addition, she has been teaching academic, career, and personal development topics to thousands of students and readers since 2004.

Outside of writing, Destiny loves and enjoys many activities: reading, weightlifting, walking, biking, traveling, football (and sports in general), dogs, animals, food, classic movies, quality and new experiences, mountain and ocean views, sleeping, plants, and nature.

Check out her work, leave a review, share your thoughts with your friends and family, and participate in a movement: **Serving others through self-education (books).**

<u>Complete the Steps To Get Free eBooks:</u>

Step 1: Go to

amazon.com/author/destinyharris

Step 2: Filter books by "Price: Low to High"

Step 3: Download available free books

...

. . .

Connect W/ Destiny S. Harris

Please reach out and stay in touch. Start a conversation today @ destinyh.com

. . .

. . .

Free Gifts!

Access courses & free eBooks at the link below:

destinyh.com

. . .

Please Leave A Review

If this book impacts you in some way, please let me know by dropping a review on it.

I write better books with **your** input.

. . .

Tell Me What You Want

I've written many books, but if you don't see what you're looking for or need, get in touch with me via my website, articles, comments, or reviews, and let me know what you're looking for so I can create it for you. I'm here to serve.

Destiny

. . .

. . .

www.ingramcontent.com/pod-product-compliance
Lightning Source LLC
Chambersburg PA
CBHW031432250726
48656CB00002B/950